Play It Down

Navigating the Challenges of Golf, Retirement, and Life

FIRST EDITION
March 2017

Dave Cox

CoxQuest Publishing
Oklahoma City, Oklahoma

Copyright © 2017 by Dave Cox

ISBN-13: 978-1543017526
ISBN-10: 1543017525

Library of Congress Control Number: 2017902680

Printed in the United States of America

DISCLAIMER

This publication is a work of fiction. Names, characters, businesses, places, and events are either the products of the author's imagination or used in a fictitious manner. Any resemblance to actual persons, living or dead, or actual events, is purely coincidental.

CoxQuest.com

Dedication

With love, I dedicate this book, my first published work of fiction, to Barbara, my incredible wife of forty years. She is the guidepost that has kept me on course through good times and bad. She is my soul mate and has made life rewarding and fun to live. And, she is my best friend, joining me often in the many and varied adventures of my life, including the one that serves as the setting for this book—the great game of golf.

To our daughter Tiffany, our son-in-law Matt, and our beautiful granddaughters, Harper and Delaney, who inspire me to explore new things every day and to enjoy life regardless of the circumstances.

Contents

Introduction

Retirement, according to the Merriam-Webster Dictionary, is defined as "withdrawal from one's position or occupation or from active working life." Now, I don't know about you, but that concept sounds pretty good to me. I've been dreaming about retiring for a very long time, but have only recently been able to make the transition from work to retirement, and, to be honest, it wasn't easy. In fact, doing so required me to make one of the most difficult decisions of my life. It seems a little out of balance to bring 40 to 50 years of work, building a career, and all that goes along with it, to an abrupt end with one simple decision.

As I became more serious about leaving the workplace for good, I began to read books, lots of books, about retirement. Most of those books were about the financial considerations. A few, very few, were about what I came to call the "other stuff." It was that other stuff that kept me up at night. And, I suspect, it keeps a lot of other folks up at night, as well. Even more frightening, though, is the prospect of someone retiring without even considering the other stuff. That other stuff is the focus of the story that unfolds in the chapters ahead.

The setting for this book is quite unique for a book on retirement, and, while based on real life experiences, revolves around a conversation among friends who regularly play golf at their local country club. It is a fable of sorts, in that it is intended to convey a valuable lesson to its main character, Jake, as well as to the readers at large, but it differs from a fable in that it's characters are people, and indirectly reflect the views, aspirations, and interests of the author.

You will soon find out what makes Jake's decision to retire so difficult, and you may be surprised to learn the real issues that Jake struggled with prior to pulling the plug on his long career.

While its intended audience is primarily people approaching retirement, the lessons conveyed in the story are universal and are applicable to all ages and all circumstances. The subject of retirement and the setting of golf were selected merely as convenient and amusing vessels for conveying the lessons. I hope you find it inspiring.

Chapter 1

The Divot

Prior to addressing the ball for his attempted hit to the sixth green, Jake bent down to move it out of a divot. It's very difficult to get a clean hit when the ball is sitting down in a divot, resting on bare ground or entangled in gnarly grass or protruding tree roots. After all, Jake and his friends were just playing for fun, so it couldn't hurt to move the ball a couple of inches. That's all, a couple of inches, no closer to the pin of course. He was playing a two-dollar Nassau with his friends—Bob, Joe and Rick—and nobody cared, at least nobody said anything.

After taking relief from the poor lie, Jake proceeded to hit the ball. Whack! Not quite to the green, but close enough, and not in the bunker. Jake hated bunker shots. He never was very good at them. After two or three attempts at launching a ball from a sandy lie, he usually tossed it onto the green—sometimes close enough to the pin for a tap-in. What could that hurt? After all, it's just a casual round with close friends.

Jake did pretty well today. His take was sixteen bucks. Not bad for a six dollar wager. He's down for the month, but he's on a roll.

Bob, Joe, Rick and Jake have played every Saturday morning for going on seven years now. They're all members of the Grey Men's League at Tempting Slopes Country Club in Bugle Springs, Georgia. That's right, the "Grey" Men's League. It ought to be "Gray," with an "a," but Joe is from England and he spelled it that way when he drafted the league rules last year. Nobody caught it at the time. You have to be sixty or older to play on the Grey Men's League, and only men are welcome. Ironically, that restriction was Jake's wife, Julie's, idea so she wouldn't have to come up with an excuse to avoid completing their foursome if one of the guys came down with the flu or something.

Considering that the Grey Men's League consisted of a grand total of four members, it doesn't seem like much of an issue if one of the wives wanted to play every once in a while. Joe's a widower, but Rick, Bob, and Jake are married and their wives all play. In fact, Julie has a lower handicap than all four of the guys. She played college golf at Georgia Tech.

If you're wondering why the Grey Men's League only has four members, well, that was kind of planned too. They really didn't want to share their special time together with others, so they all agreed not to ask anyone else to join. Truth be known, the only reason they even set up the league in the first place was for tax purposes. Joe was a financial planner back in England and he convinced the others that they could deduct their membership dues on their income taxes—as a business expense.

Following the round, Jake and the others convened in the men's locker room—another reason for the "men only" provision—to tally up their scores and divvy up the pot. And, of course, to wind down over a cold beer—a weekly tradition for the group. The rest of the pot—eight dollars— was split between Bob and Joe.

This day was different, though. For some reason, Rick seemed a bit agitated. He was shut out today, but he'd gone a round or two before without winning anything, and he'd never gotten upset.

"You okay, Rick?" asked Jake. "You seem a little down today."

"Yeah," said Rick. "I'm fine, just tired."

But, everything wasn't fine. He just didn't want to say anything—at least not now. They finished their beers and left.

At home, Jake told Julie, his wife of 37 years, about Rick's peculiar behavior during the day's round. He was worried about his long-time friend, and couldn't let it go. Rick had battled prostate cancer a few years back and Jake was afraid that it might have returned. Julie, a registered nurse at Mercy General—and the level-headed one in the family—told Jake to not jump to any conclusions. That was one of Jake's many weaknesses. He let his imagination run wild sometimes.

"Just keep an eye on him," said Julie. "If it was about losing at golf today, he'll be fine next week, especially if he wins something. If it's something more serious, he'll probably be down then too."

The following Saturday, Rick called Jake a few minutes before their standing tee-time to let him know he wouldn't be playing. He said he wasn't feeling well. Jake was even more concerned now that his friend's cancer might have come back. He didn't want to say anything, but it made sense now why Rick was so down following last week's round.

Jake quickly phoned Julie to see if she could fill in for Rick, but she was quick to remind him that women weren't allowed to play in the Grey Men's League. The threesome played on, but things were different without Rick.

"We may have to change that rule, guys," hinted Jake. No one responded.

Hole number one went about as well as could be expected. None of the guys ever warm up before a round, so the first few holes are generally, shall we say, handicap enhancers. Bob says he's only got so many swings left in his decrepit old body and he 'ain't gonna waste 'em on practice.' Bob's real problem, however, is his weight. If you could catch him before breakfast, and still in his skivvies, he'd probably weigh in at about 280, maybe 300. I'm surprised he can swing a club at all.

The day's round was pretty much a carbon copy of last week's round, and the week before that, and the week before that. Nothing ever changes much. The only excitement, most days, is Joe's drives—long, but unpredictable. When I see Joe hit the ball, I'm always reminded of the joke about the gorilla that hit his first tee shot 400 yards. His drive was so intimidating that his competitors conceded the round. Then the gorilla hit his second shot—400 yards, then his third shot—400 yards. If he ever managed to get on a green, his putt was, you guessed it, 400 yards.

It shouldn't be any surprise that Joe hits a ball so long. He's the youngest of the group and the fittest, by far. He's a bit stocky—buff in his own words—but strong as an ox. He lives on a farm west of town and spends a lot of time working outside.

Jake is the odd man of the group. He probably tips the scales at maybe 135—soaking wet. He can't hit the ball very far so he relies on his accuracy, and, let's be honest, he cheats, sort of. When he reaches his ball in the fairway, he moves it to a better lie. If it's in a divot, he moves it out of the divot and tees it up on a nice tuft of grass. If it's behind a tree, he moves it. I suppose 'improving your lie' is okay in a friendly game, but he does it all the time, and he wins a lot because of it. He cheats—I don't know how else to put it.

In golf, as in life, you generally have a choice as to how you approach challenges that come your way. You can "play it down" or you can "play it up." For those of you unfamiliar with golf terminology, to "play it down" means to play the ball as it lies. If that means hitting it out of a divot, then hitting it out of a divot it shall be. Problem is, that's not as easy as it might seem. The challenges, as well as the nerves required to perform such a shot, are equally unsettling when confronted with any number of less-than-perfect lies. The results— not to be confused with the consequences— however, can be significantly different depending on how you approach the shot. The results are what happens to the "ball." The consequences are what happens to "you."

I should explain at this point the reason why Jake, and most amateur golfers for that matter, choose to improve their lie before hitting the ball. While the reason may be obvious, the possible consequences are quite evasive and can have long-term implications. Golfers improve their lie to increase their chances of getting a "clean hit." A clean hit is when the golf club strikes the golf ball in the sweet spot without interference from confounding elements such as grass, sand or roots. The "sweet spot" is the place on the face of the golf club that has been engineered to produce the most efficient and effective launch of the golf ball when struck by the golf club at the bottom of the downswing—the impact. The results can, and generally are, much better when a clean hit is achieved. I'll get to the consequences later.

The divot in this story is a metaphor for the challenges that we are confronted with in life. To "play it up" means to use artificial or temporary measures to get past difficulties that we face each and every day of our lives. While the immediate results may be better and much easier to accept, the long-term implications can be devastating.

With the Spring Four-Man Scramble now just two weeks away, the group decided to put a little extra effort into every shot. Concentrate on stance, grip, swing, and especially on reading the greens. Tournaments are generally won by those with the best short game. Today, the guys will suspend the Nassau and will help each other with every aspect of their respective games. They'll offer constructive criticism to each other, whether requested or not. They'll suggest more effective approaches when appropriate. They'll concentrate on "course management" and develop a winning strategy for the tournament. And, they'll all read everyone's putts—an approach that they could legally use in a scramble.

With Rick out, the threesome moved around the course pretty quickly. They always try to get a tee time between 9:00 and 9:30 AM. That puts them just behind the early morning 'serious' golfers that keep up a good pace, and just ahead of the 11:00 AM old men's open play group that schedules fivesomes and tend to drag a round out to five hours or more, another reason for forming their own league and limiting the membership.

When they got to the turn, Julie was waiting on the 10th tee box with fresh muffins and hot coffee for everyone. And, just in case she was asked again to join them, she conveniently had her golf clubs in the trunk of her car. She finds it hard to resist an offer to play, even with the guys.

"Care to join us, Julie?" offered Joe. "We could use some tips from a pro. We're trying to get our game in shape for the Spring Scramble. Jake may have told you."

"I'd love to, Joe," said Julie. "Thanks for asking. It'll just take a second to grab my clubs."

Jake was riding with Joe, so he and Bob switched places so Julie and Jake could share a cart. They were off on hole 10 before the group behind them was even in sight.

Julie had another reason for wanting to join the group at the turn. After Jake phoned her earlier, she decided to call Roxanne, Rick's wife, to see how Rick was feeling. Roxanne hesitated at first, but then, in a low voice, said Rick was fine, that he was just tired. When pressed, Roxanne hesitated again, started to say something, then repeated that he was just tired. Now Julie was concerned, as was Jake, that something more serious was troubling Rick.

Julie led off on ten with a great drive—down the middle and long—especially for a lady. She outdrove everyone but Joe.

"Great drive, Julie," said Joe.

"Thanks, Joe."

"Nice drive honey," Jake whispered as Julie slid back into the cart.

The back nine went a little slower with four playing, but they still managed to stay ahead of the group behind them. No one asked Julie for advice on their game and Julie didn't offer. Ironically, the men's level of play actually dropped a little with Julie joining the group. No logical reason for that, but I suspect it's a male ego thing or bruised pride.

Following the round, Julie joined a couple of her friends that were having lunch in the dining room and the guys retreated to the men's locker room for their weekly ritual.

Next week, they'll play an actual scramble format in preparation for the tournament. In a four-man scramble, each player hits his own tee shot. The team—the foursome in this case—then decides which of the four tee shots is best and they each play their second shot from that location. In accordance with the rules, each player will place his ball within one club length of the resting place of the selected tee shot, no closer to the hole, and hit away. Being able to place your ball during a scramble is a huge advantage over traditional play since you can place it on a nice tuft of grass, teed-up so to speak, assuring good contact with the ball. As with the tee shot, the group then selects the best second shot and each player hits their third shot from that location, playing it up. This approach is continued until the ball is holed out, even on the green. I should point out, however, that in a scramble scenario, playing the ball up doesn't offer any advantage over the other teams since everyone will be doing the same.

Chapter 2

The Safety Pin

With only one week remaining before the tournament, the guys were psyched. The pressure was mounting as the group approached the first tee for their last practice round. They'd play a scramble format today, as planned. It was nice having Rick back in the group, but he still seemed a little down. He just wasn't his usual self. Jake couldn't put his finger on it, but he still wasn't comfortable confronting him.

A scramble, especially one played during a tournament, brings out a different demeanor in players. They often approach it with a false sense of calm knowing that every shot, their shot in particular, doesn't have to be perfect. There's always the other guys to cover for your mistakes. Life can be that way too. Everyone makes mistakes. The smart ones among us learn from those mistakes and do better next time. The others assume that someone—their boss, their spouse, their teammate—will cover for them if things go awry. In life, as in golf, you should always strive to do your best, regardless of the situation, accept the outcome gracefully, enjoy your successes, and learn from your mistakes.

"It's your honor, Rick, since you were out last week," Jake insisted as he pulled his driver out of his golf bag. "Down the middle."

In a scramble, everyone in the group roots for everyone else since it's a team event. As the game unfolds and each player's strengths begin to emerge, a game strategy will be adopted. For example, if Rick is consistently hitting the most accurate drives this week—down the middle of the fairway—they may designate him to hit the first tee shot on each hole. If Rick gets a good hit, that frees up the rest of them to pull out all stops and try to hit it even better—longer and straighter—even if they can't. It's that male ego thing again. The long-hitter, clearly Joe in the group, will go last, and assuming that they have a good drive already in the fairway, he'll unleash all he has to offer. When Joe's "in the zone," he's capable of unleashing a 320-yard drive. Where it lands in relation to the fairway, however, is another matter altogether. Long isn't always good—unless your wedge game is solid. Long John (PGA Tour professional John Daly) used to ride that wave a lot. He'd drive the ball 350 yards or more with little regard to where it might land. Even if his ball landed in the rough or in an adjacent fairway, he could usually launch it up and over any confounding obstacles—trees, hazards or buildings—and get it on or close to the green. Most of the time that strategy worked well for John. He's tamed it down a bit now that he's on the Champions Tour.

Rick's drive came to rest in the fairway, just left of center. He hit it a little fat so it came up quite a bit short of where they needed it to be for a good approach to the green.

"Nice hit Rick," proclaimed Bob. "Down the middle, as usual. Does that ever get boring?"

"Always, but I'd rather be bored than in the pond. Just wish I could hit it a little longer—like I could when I was younger."

"Not a problem," Joe announced with an air of confidence. "At least not today. Fortunately, you boys have me to carry you."

Bob was next to hit.

"Nice drive Bob," Jake commented, as he approached the tee box. Jake seems unable to just play a quiet round of golf. He's the guy—you all have one—that compliments everyone on every shot. It's nice for a while, but it gets really annoying after a few holes.

Jake was next up. His drive landed right of center and a little longer than Rick's. It'd work if Joe missed his queue for some reason.

Well, Joe didn't miss his queue. He hit a monstrous drive, and down the middle this time. In fact, they were looking at only a wedge to get home from where his ball came to rest—maybe 60 yards to the pin, at most.

As the practice round progressed, Joe continued to hold steady with his drives—long and straight. If he can do that next week, they've got a good chance at placing in the money. When it comes to "carding" a low score, the short game is usually the most important part of any round, but a drive in the fairway and within reach of the green, especially on a par-5, is a huge advantage. At their age, the greens aren't reachable in regulation as much as they used to be.

The highlight of the round came on the seventh hole when Joe decided to go for the green. It's about 330 yards from the gray tees, but reachable by Joe under certain conditions, notably a strong tail wind, as was the case today. Rick's drive was in pretty good shape, so Joe's attempt at this juncture was without much risk.

"It's all yours Joe," said Rick. "The green's open. Let the big dog eat."

I don't think I've ever seen a swing as strained as Joe's was on the seventh tee that day. He grunted on the backswing. He grunted on the downswing. And, he grunted at impact. The ball came off the face of the driver like nothing I'd ever seen, or heard, before. I don't know how they can make golf clubs that can sustain that much force. It actually arched upward as it climbed away from the tee box. What a sight to see—assuming you could even see it.

Just as the ball began its decent—or rather its reentry—our attention was diverted from the area in which we were looking, specifically around the green where we were expecting to see the ball land, to a yell of jubilation, we thought, coming from the tee box. What we all saw when we turned to the tee was nothing less than shocking. What we heard was not a yell of jubilation at all, but rather a scream of desperation. There was Joe, bending over gripping the waistband of his slacks. The zipper, the button, and the belt had all snapped under the immense strain generated during Joe's savage swing. His slacks had dropped to the turf and he was left mooning a full house of members and guests dining in the clubhouse. What happened next surprised us even more.

"Anyone got a safety pin?" asked Joe calmly, as though nothing had happened. None of us could answer his query—we were all laid out on the ground rolling in fits of laughter. Once we composed ourselves, Jake got up, reached into his pants pocket, pulled out a safety pin and handed it to Joe. Not just any safety pin—a giant safety pin. It was at least three inches long—perfectly suited for the task at hand.

"Seriously!" commented Bob. "What the heck are you doing with a giant safety pin in your pocket Jake? Is there something we should know?"

"It depends," chided Jake. "Pun intended."

"Good one Jake."

Joe quickly repaired his slacks, carefully slid into his waiting golf cart, and slowly pulled away from the tee box.

Over the next several holes, the guys would periodically and spontaneously break out in laughter as they recalled Joe's seventh hole debacle. To this day, no one knows why Jake had that giant safety pin in his pocket.

From time to time, things—unusual things—happen that have no logical explanation. There's lots of speculation as to why such things happen, but it's only that—speculation. Why Jake had that giant safety pin in his pocket that day is anyone's guess. I suspect that if you asked Jake, he'd tell you he didn't even know. Perhaps there's a sixth sense that man has not yet discovered. There's a lot of evidence that suggests such a realm of possibility exists. Perhaps, that giant safety pin lying on Jake's bureau had garnered his attention that particular morning a little more than past mornings—just enough for Jake to grab it and put it in his pocket, in case it might be needed—better safe than sorry. Some might even attribute the occurrence to Divine intervention. Be it as it may. Regardless of the reason for Jake's unexplained decision that particular morning, and the unusual turn of events that day that benefited from his decision, it might be best to just accept it for what it is and move on.

Golf, and life for that matter, is often interrupted by unexplained events or circumstances that help or hinder our approach to a particular situation. That's just life. If it makes us feel better, we tend to categorize it as normal, but if it hinders us, we typically get upset about the "unfortunate" turn of events and try to justify the results as bad luck. The truth is, that's also life. It might be best to accept both good and bad as realities of life, approach them with equal vigilance and make the best of the situation. I'm not suggesting that you just lay back and let things happen, good or bad. I'm only recognizing that fact that they do happen, and it might be better to approach them in a positive manner rather than categorize them as good or bad, and react accordingly. Contrary to popular belief, the choice is yours. Chose wisely and you may be surprised at the outcome.

It took a few holes for them to get back into the rhythm of the game, but they were on a mission. They really wanted to do well in next week's tournament, so they tried to keep their minds on the task at hand.

Joe reached the seventh green with his drive and continued to hit great shots all day. Bob putted the lights out today. He had seven one-putts, including one forty-footer. Let's hope that holds for the tournament. As with the tee shots, they'll assign players to their strengths accordingly. Since Bob was putting so well today, they'll have him putt last at the beginning of the tournament, after watching the other guys' putts. The roll of the ball and speed of the green is much easier to predict if you can watch someone else putt before you. Even better if you can watch three putts prior to yours. If someone else emerges as the star putter next week, they'll make a change in the putting order. Same for the drive.

As for Rick and Jake, well, they were playing about average today. Hopefully, they'll be able to contribute a little more next week. Regardless of today's stats, playing order for the tournament will be determined depending on how everyone's playing at the time—and even that could change during the round. Joe will most likely be the mop-up driver on most holes, due to his length, but the rest is up in the air until the round begins.

"Eight-under guys," Jake shared with the others following the round. "Not too bad, but that won't bring home the bacon next week. The winning score last year was eleven-under. We've got a ways to go. We're so close. We've just got to find the missing key. Want to play a practice round sometime this week?"

"Practice! We've been practicing for seven years," Bob shouted, with a little disgust in his voice. "One more round ain't gonna make any difference at this point. We'll be ready—as ready as we can be. Besides, I promised Betty I'd clean out the garage this week. Better pass."

"How about you, Rick?" asked Jake, hoping for an opportunity to probe Rick about his recent behavior. "Want to play this week? I'll get us a tee-time."

"Guess I'd better pass too, Jake. Thanks anyway," said Rick, in a less than enthusiastic tone. "See you next week. We'll find your missing key then—I promise."

If there's any weakness at all in the group, it's in their ability to communicate—or rather the lack thereof. Jake talks too much. Rick doesn't talk enough. Joe only talks when he's got something important to say. As for Bob, well Bob's kind of the arbitrator for the group. He intercedes when there's a disagreement, and tries to get everyone's mind back on the game. So far, it's worked pretty well. As you know, the group's been playing every Saturday for over seven years. Something must be working. Bob will have his work cut out for him next week—communicating could just be the key Jake is looking for.

Chapter 3

Tournament Day

Tournament day had arrived, and everyone showed up as excited as ever. Even Rick was in a good mood compared to the last few weeks. I'm assuming he had gotten good news following his last doctor appointment.

"Hole 7," exclaimed Bob, as they approached their carts and read off their starting position. Most amateur tournaments these days have a "shotgun start" so everyone starts and completes their round at the same time. That works out best for the awards ceremony, and lunch, if provided—no one has to wait too long for either. With eighteen teams signed up, every hole will be full.

Hole 7 is the signature hole at Tempting Slopes. It's a short par-4 dogleg right, over water, with a very shallow green. We call it "the safety pin." To discourage long-hitters from going for it on their drive, the green is protected on the front left by a deep bunker and slopes away to the back.

Even if you hit the green, getting it to hold takes real talent and a little luck. We, of course, had an advantage. We had reached the green the previous week, so we knew what we were capable of.

"That suits me just fine," proclaimed Joe. "If one of you duffers can get your ball in play, I can go for the green. I know that's asking a lot with today's wind, but it'd sure be nice to start the tournament off with a birdie." No one mentioned what had happened the previous week at the seventh hole, but I suspect Jake had a safety pin in his pocket, just in case the unthinkable happened—again.

"Guess you're first up, Rick. Bore us," insisted Jake. As expected, Rick's drive was down the middle, a little short but only about 85 yards to the pin.

"We're good, guys. Go for it," insisted Rick. And, "go for it" they did. Jake hit second—a long and high fading slice deep into the lake. Bob's wasn't much better—long and strait—strait through the fairway into the trees on the left, that is. Strange things happen when you crank it up a notch with no regard for results—hoping for a once-in-a-lifetime hit. Only about 60 yards to the pin, but it'd take a nicely struck sand wedge to clear the trees and drop onto the front of the green, allowing enough distance to the pin for the roll out. None of these guys had "backspin" in their repertoire. Thank goodness we've got Rick's ball in the fairway.

Next up—mop-up man.

Wham! "Looks good. Great hit, Joe. On line. Is it long enough? Go, go, yes—no!" as commentated by Jake, as the ball landed just short of the green. Great hit, but short on hole 7 means a trip to the beach—the sand trap. What a downer to begin the round. It sure looked good when Joe hit it.

"Okay guys," Jake tried to console the others. "I know it looks bad, but don't forget we can "play it up" even in the sand, plus we've each got two mulligans. I say we take Joe's ball. We're pretty good from the sand. I think we can get closer to the pin from the bunker than from 85 yards out."

"Pretty good from the sand?" inquired Bob. "What have you been smoking this morning, Jake? The only time you've been good out of the sand was that time you scooped the ball up with your gin glass and tossed it into the hole for an eagle."

After a brief deliberation, everyone agreed, some hesitantly, to take Joe's ball. Rick hit first and landed just past the pin, but it ran off the back of the green. It's a tough up-and-down from there. Bob skulled his attempt, landing the ball about 40 yards over the green.

"Take your time, Jake," grumbled Joe, hoping for a good shot so the pressure wouldn't be on him to salvage his drive. Jake hit it thin and slammed the ball hard into the bank, just below the lip. Now the pressure was on Joe. Joe has the lowest handicap, so it only stands to reason that their best chance for a sand-save still remained. And, they all still have mulligans, if needed.

"We really need this, Joe," insisted Bob. "No pressure. Sorry, but if we leave this hole with only a par, we're done. Everybody else will likely birdie this hole."

Joe backed off, allowing Bob to rant for a few seconds. Bob was good at that, really good. He'd settle down in a few seconds. "Bob, would you please shut up. I'm trying to concentrate. It's only the first hole. We're not done yet," Joe insisted, trying to keep his cool and settle Bob down at the same time.

Swoofff! That's the sound you want to hear when hitting out of the sand. Joe's ball barely cleared the lip, ran out the slope from the left, and crept ever so slowly toward the hole. The next sound was the rattle of the ball as it hit the bottom of the cup.

"Awesome!" shouted Bob. "Never a doubt."

"Way to go," added Jake. "Nice eagle."

Rick patted Joe on the back, plucked his ball from the cup and offered it to him as if the hole-out was expected.

"When you're good, you're good. Two-under after one," touted Jake. "Nice start."

The next two holes were played in one under par, making them three-under at the turn. The "turn" is normally the crossover from the front nine to the back nine, but since they started on seven, the turn today came after only three holes. Three-under after only three holes is a great start to any tournament.

Chapter 4

The Turn

"Anybody want a beer?" queried Bob. It's standard procedure to hit the bar at the turn. Of course, the "turn" came two hours earlier today than normal for the group.

"Are you kidding," Jake asked in a puzzled tone of voice. "It's ten o'clock—in the morning. And, we do need to keep our wits about us today if we have any chance of winning."

"It's five o'clock somewhere," reasoned Bob, as he headed for the clubhouse.

"Good grief, Jake. Lighten up," insisted Joe. "If Bob wants a beer, let him have a beer. Last I checked, he was an adult, capable of making his own decisions. Assuming Betty isn't around to make them for him, that is." Everyone laughed, except Jake.

"Lighten up? Are you kidding—it's a tournament, guys." I thought we were going to be serious about this," Jake clamored as the others faded into the doorway of the clubhouse for a

29

quick restroom break. Restroom breaks come often at their age.

Jake was a little on edge today—more so than normal. Thankfully, it wasn't affecting his game—at least not yet.

Rick was still driving the ball nicely so he'd continue to lead off. Next up—hole 10, or 4, depending on your perspective.

The tenth hole is a 520 yard par-5 dogleg right. It's reachable in two with two great shots. That's very doable in a scramble format. In fact, a birdie is expected on number 10. A great chance to move to four-under.

"Where's Jake? asked Rick as he waited to hit his drive.

"He seems a little distracted today," offered Bob. "Hope I didn't upset him by getting a beer so early."

"I don't think that's it. He's been under a lot of pressure at work lately. His boss upped his quota. He's thinking about changing jobs," said Bob.

"Again?" asked Rick. "I thought he was planning on retiring soon."

"He talks a lot about retiring, but I'm not sure he's ready," offered Joe. "It's a big decision and there's no going back once you pull the plug. I've been retired for eight years now, and I can honestly say there have been times, lots of times, that I thought I had made a big mistake retiring so early. There's a lot more to consider than finances. I can tell you that. Everyone talks about the finances. But, that's only one aspect to consider."

"Here he comes guys," Rick announced under his breath. "Did you get lost, Jake?"

"Distracted." Jake admitted. "Julie and I play so many 9-hole tournaments with the Couples League that I instinctively went to the first tee after the turn. Sorry."

"Joe said you've been thinking about retiring. Any truth to that, or is he just trying to start another vicious rumor?" asked Bob. "If you retire, you could join Joe and me on Tuesdays. We're always looking for new members for the Tuesday Boomer's League. So, what's up? Are you thinking about retirement, or not?"

"I've been 'thinking' about retirement since I got my first job at sixteen. Doesn't everyone?"

"So, what's stopping you?" Rick asked, as he approached the number 10 tee box.

Whack! Rick launched his drive down the middle and long. He looked like Matt Kuchar picking up his tee and walking off the tee box before his drive even hits the ground. The stage was now set for Joe regardless of what Jake and Bob did.

"I don't know—the uncertainties, I guess. Things are pretty good at the office right now, but I'm not getting any younger, and there are a lot of things on my To Do list that conflict with full-time employment."

"Like the Tuesday Boomer's League," quipped Bob.

"Huh? There's more to life than golf, Bob," Jake offered, after Rick's drive on ten.

"I know that," Bob responded.

"I do want to play more golf, that's for sure," said Jake. I think I can get my handicap down to single digits if I work at it. Julie and I want to do a lot of traveling, too. And, we want to spend more time with the grandkids while they still want to spend time with us. But, all of that stuff will have to wait until I retire, and I'm just not ready, not quite yet."

"What are you waiting for?" asked Bob. "As you said, you're not getting any younger. If it's the money, Joe can stake you until you hit the lottery."

"Money's a factor of course, but I think we'll be okay if the market doesn't crash in the next twenty years, Congress doesn't do away with Social Security, we don't have any catastrophic health issues, or . . ."

"Hold on, Jake." Joe interrupted, as he pulled away from the others for a more private conversation with Jake. "I see your problem— you're paranoid. If you dwell long enough on everything that can go wrong, you'll find something that will go wrong, guaranteed. You've got to be more positive, man. It's a big change, believe me—I've been there. But, everyone has to stop working at some point, unless they work until they die. I doubt that that is what you want."

"It was difficult for me to cut lose eight years ago," continued Joe, "but it was definitely the right decision. And, believe me, there have been a few times since then that I questioned my decision to retire so early. I didn't have to—I chose to. I wanted to retire while I was still healthy enough to enjoy life. It's that simple. After I lost Madge, all that mattered was my health. We had dreams of travel, spending time together, even playing golf at some of the world's great courses—Pebble Beach, the Old Course at St. Andrews. All of that changed when Madge got sick. She made me promise to take care of myself. Do some of the things we talked about. Follow our dreams. That last year with Madge was tough—really tough—and I decided right then and there that I wasn't going to work a day longer than absolutely necessary. I decided that I would take Madge's advice and enjoy what life I had left, and she's been with me ever since—on every adventure—every step of the way."

Bob was up next. His drive faded to the right and came to rest behind a grove of trees that's hard to get around.

"Are you guys going to play or talk?" Bob yelled to Jake and Joe, as he tried to pull them back into the game.

"Sorry guys," Joe replied, as he and Jake moved toward the tee box.

"Wow. I had no idea Joe," Jake said, as he struggled to maintain his composure. "I often wondered why you've never talked about being married before you came to the states. I figured you'd share what you wanted to share."

"Well, now you know, Jake. I'm just a lonely old man trying to stay alive. Keep this between us, okay."

"Sure. You may be right about my retirement." Jake agreed, with some reservation. "It may be paranoia. I've read about a dozen books on retirement over the past year or so and there's a lot to consider. And, to be honest, you just added one—a big one. None of those books talked about enjoying life while you still have your health. Most of them only cover the financial considerations. It's all the 'other stuff' that worries me—loss of identity, loss of camaraderie, lack of purpose, boredom, even depression. Money is just one factor to consider."

Jake was right. Most of the books about retirement only talk about finances, but a few of the better ones talk about the less obvious things that people confront when they leave their job behind—the "other stuff" Jake alluded to—things that they don't even think about beforehand.

"Maybe it wasn't such a good idea to read all of those books," Jake continued. "Sure, I learned a lot about preparing for retirement, coping with all of the downsides of leaving behind what you've done all of your life, dealing with all the things that not having a job brings, but . . ."

"There you go again, Jake. It's good to learn about the challenges that others have faced in retirement, but you can't obsess over them or you'll never retire, regardless of how prepared you are."

"Come on guys. We're getting backed up," warned Bob, as the group behind them pulled up to the number 10 tee box

Jake hit a draw about 220 into the left rough, leaving them with a much longer shot to the green than Rick's drive. The group in front of them was out of sight so they'd try to speed up a bit. The marshal comes around often and they sure didn't want to get dinged for slow play.

With Rick's drive perfectly placed, Joe stepped up to his ball with the confidence that only Joe could have. Some call it arrogance, but it truly is confidence. The difference, if you are wondering, will be evident in the outcome of Joe's hit. The tenth hole will likely be birdied by several teams over the course of the tournament, so he'd need a good hit. Ten is a dogleg right, so he aimed over the trees even though it'd take a monster drive to clear them.

Wham! "Great hit Joe," Jake said. "That pretty much assures us of a birdie here. We can't be more than 220 out."

"Not so fast, Jake," cautioned Joe. "We're not in the hole yet."

"Thankfully, money isn't an issue," resumed Jake, as he jumped into the golf cart with Joe. "We've paid in to Julie's 401K for twenty-five years and it's done pretty well, especially in the late 90s. It's the "other stuff" that keeps me from pulling the plug.

"I'm confused, Jake." Joe interrupted. "You say you're okay financially. You say it's all the 'other stuff' that bothers you. What specifically is it about the 'other stuff' that bothers you?"

"I don't know—the unknowns I guess."

"Okay, let's look at them one at a time. First of all, you've said many times that you don't have any friends at work. Is that true?"

"Pretty much—no one that I socialize with."

"So, let's scratch the 'camaraderie' thing," said Joe. "How about 'too much free time.' I can tell you from personal experience that you will find plenty of things to do. Everyone is concerned about having nothing to fill their days once they retire, but those same people, following their retirement, will tell you that they now have even less free time. Hasn't Julie started her "Honey Do" list yet?"

"Sure, but that's only good for a few weeks at most," explained Jake.

"And, your daughter?" asked Bob. "If she's anything like my kids, she'll have you signed up as her full-time handyman before your final paycheck hits the bank."

Jake was first to hit his second shot from where Joe's drive came to rest. He hit it really well but it still came up about 60 yards short of the green. Bob and Rick weren't back yet from retrieving their tee shots, so Joe stepped up to the tee. He was spot on with his approach shot, landing about ten yards short right and running up onto the green and curving left toward the pin like a bird dog on a hot trail. Bob and Rick, realizing that they couldn't reach the green on their best day, drove on without stopping to hit their second shot to make up some time.

"Come on guys, concentrate. We're playing a tournament—remember," quipped Jake, as they walked onto the tenth green.

"Concentrate?" shouted Bob. "We're just trying to pick up the pace. You're the ones that need to concentrate. Your little sidebar conversations are the reason were behind in the first place."

"Okay, I deserve that. Can we just concentrate on golf now?" Jake pleaded. "I really thought we had a chance coming into this tournament. I doubt that any one of you jerks even know what our score is. Any guesses?"

"Three-under," shouted Rick. "Five if you make this putt."

"Consider it in. Let me see, hmmm, maybe six inches outside the cup, right to left. What do you think guys?" queried Jake.

The first guy up in a scramble is the guinea pig. His putt serves as a guide for everyone else. The later in the sequence you putt, the better your chances of holing it. Staging the best putter last improves the chances of the team, as a whole, making the putt. If, like me, your group always puts you first in the sequence, don't fret—they aren't necessarily telling you that you are the worst putter. They are just acknowledging the fact that their chances are better if they see someone else putt first. Your best response to being placed first on the roster for putting is to hole the darn thing.

The life lesson here is that your chances of success are greatly improved if you have the benefit of observing someone else first, not just in putting but in most things that you do. Learn from 'their' mistakes. Of course, you don't always have that option, so you must approach every challenge as if it is yours alone, as if you are first up. And, if you do make a mistake, that's okay. That's how you learn. That's how we all learn.

"Sounds about right to me," agreed Bob. "Interesting pin placement. This green is always fast, but it's really fast back here. Not much more than a tap in."

"I don't know—too easy and it'll break a lot more than six inches. I think I've got a better chance if I give it a good tap—back of the cup."

"You'd better hit the back of the cup or you'll end up twenty feet past the hole."

Life, like golf, presents us with many challenges. Most of them can be approached in more than one way—firm and to the point, soft and easy, or something in between. The key to successfully navigating life, and the golf course, is to CONSIDER all of your options, CHOOSE the course of action that offers you the greatest odds for success, COMMIT to the decision you make, and CONFIDENTLY EXECUTE your choice. I call it the 4Cs Model. In Jake's case, "firm and to the point" made the most sense. Bob is a "soft and easy" kind of player. Either approach will work given the proper execution.

Jake missed, by the way. He hit it a little too firm. It slid by just above the cup and rolled off the front of the green, just as Bob had predicted. Rick was next up. Same approach—same result. Now it was Bob's turn—soft and easy. Close, but it slid by as well, just below the cup. Fortunately, it came to rest about four feet below the cup, leaving a fairly easy putt back up the hill. Joe's putt lipped out, leaving a short tap-in for their birdie.

A scramble format is the ultimate opportunity to "play the ball up." In fact, it's in the rules to do so. Unfortunately, playing the ball up, while making it easier to hit the ball cleanly, robs a player of his opportunity to hit the ball as it lies. If you don't play the ball down occasionally, the game is much more difficult when you have to play by the rules, and so is life. Life is complicated even more in that we generally don't have the option of taking the easy way out, at least not without consequences.

A scramble format also offers a player the benefit of observing others attempting what he or she is about to attempt, presenting them with a real-life experience as an innocent bystander, on which to base his or her own approach. Unfortunately, life doesn't always work that way.

There may not be an easy way out. Learning from others' mistakes, or from your own for that matter, may not be an option. Sometimes we just have to step up to the ball and hit it. That's why it is so important to adopt the 4Cs model—CONSIDER, CHOOSE, COMMIT, and CONFIDENTLY EXECUTE.

Chapter 5

The "D" Wedge

As the round continued, birdies were less frequent than the group had hoped for and the group's confidence was fading. They parred eleven, birdied twelve, and parred thirteen, fourteen and fifteen. Now facing the short par-5 sixteen, they all felt that their chances of placing in the money rested heavily on a birdie here, a birdie on eighteen and a birdie on three. If they could do that, they'd be very satisfied with their round—they'd be eight-under in the clubhouse. Birdies on any of the other holes would be icing on the cake.

As Rick approached the tee, Jake reluctantly pointed out that they'd need to use Rick's and Bob's tee shots on at least four of the last nine holes. The rules, which they had conveniently overlooked, required the use of at least two drives from each player on the team over the course of the tournament. The group had used Joe's drive on every hole except eight and fifteen, where Jake's drives were used, so they both were good to go, but Rick and Bob still needed two drives each.

Hopefully, either Rick or Bob would have playable drives here, and on holes seventeen, one, two, five and six. That'd leave holes eighteen, three and four for them to take advantage of Joe's length. He can easily drive the green on eighteen and four, and three is reachable in two if he cuts the corner.

As expected, Joe's drive was, by far, the longest on sixteen, and in the fairway. They sure wanted to play his ball, but to appease Jake, and to follow the rules, they'd use Bob's tee shot. It was about 60 yards behind Joe's, and in the fairway. If Joe hit his second shot pure, he could get them close to the green, something no one else could do from that far out. He pulled his 3-wood slightly and landed about 30 yards short and left—a short chip to the front pin. With any luck, they could get up and down from there for their much needed birdie.

Jake pulled out his putter—his trusty "D" wedge—appropriately name because of its mallet design, and headed for Joe's ball. Bob and Rick elected to use their wedge, while Joe would go with his eight iron. Interesting mix of strategies—a putt, two lobs, and a bump-and-run—for what appeared to be a fairly simple shot.

That's the interesting thing about golf. We are often faced with challenges on the course that appear to be fairly simple, but, upon execution, prove to be quite difficult. Kind of sounds like life, doesn't it. Don't ever confuse simple with easy. They can be, and often are, at opposite ends of the spectrum.

As it turned out, both Bob and Rick chunked their chip shots, Joe's bump-and-run ran a little too far, and Jake's magic touch stopped just short of the cup—another tap-in for birdie. I believe it was Arnie—the King—who said: "The worst putt always beats the best chip." God rest his soul.

Seventeen, due to its length, is not really a birdie hole, so par there was good. But eighteen is a different story. It's a dogleg right with an elevated tee box and an elevated green separated by a gently sloping valley, and it's reachable by many of the longer hitters in the tournament. The group really needed a birdie there to stay in the hunt. If Joe hits over the trees on the right and avoids the three bunkers protecting the green, he should be close if not on. It's about 320 from today's tee position—well within Joe's range with the wind coming from behind. Rick, Bob, and Jake all had pretty good drives, but everyone's money was riding on Joe.

"Come on Joe," rooted Bob. "You've got this. Get it close and we'll take it from there."

"Wind's from behind, Joe," instructed Jake. "And, a little from the left. It'll take all you've got. Aim for the tall cottonwood and it should be good."

Jake just couldn't help himself. He had to offer his expert advice. He knows it's not welcome. He knows he's not offering anything the others don't already know. But, he just can't help himself. That's just Jake. The others have come to accept it, but they still get annoyed at him every once in awhile.

Whack! Joe gave it all he had. The sound of his driver hitting the ball was deafening. He hits a Cobra driver that he bought from Jake last year and he uses a high compression ball. That combination makes for a lot of noise on impact. In fact, the high pitch "boing" of the Cobra is the reason Jake sold it to Joe in the first place. He hit it okay, it just hurt his ears every time he used it, literally.

"Nice hit, Joe," said Bob. "I think you did it. I think it's there."

There's one thing I failed to mention in my earlier discussion about the 4Cs model. There's one more factor that is critical in life and occasionally comes in handy on the links as well—faith. That's right—faith. None of the guys could actually see where Joe's ball landed, but they all knew where it needed to be. Only Joe 'knew' it was there. Joe had faith. In life, faith gives us the strength to accept our circumstances knowing that everything will work out for the best. It stifles worry and disbelief. It's not always obvious, but it's certainly comforting. Faith is often confused with religion. Certainly, Christianity, as well as most other religions, has a strong basis in faith, but faith goes far beyond religion. Faith is the ability, whether you are a religious person or not, to have unquestionable confidence in someone or something, regardless of the circumstances.

As the group approached the green, they were all scouring the landscape, especially the green, for Joe's ball. There's a lot going on around the eighteenth green, so anything is possible. It could be in one of the three bunkers guarding the front and right side. If it went long, it could have caught the cart path behind the green and rolled all the way down to the first tee—some fifty yards away. If it came up a little short, it could very easily have caught the slope up to the green and rolled thirty to forty yards back down the fairway. Then there's the parking lot long and right. One or two of the guys were even questioning whether or not they'd find the ball at all. If that was the case, they'd have to play one of the other balls, probably Rick's, who's in the fairway—a long ways out, but nevertheless in the fairway. The lesson here is quite simple—have faith in the best result, but be prepared for the worst. If the result turns out to be less than you'd hoped for, then it's time to call upon your faith again that it'll work out.

"I found it," yelled Bob. It was a few inches short of the right-hand bunker, settled down deep in the rough, on the outside lip—a tough hit for anyone.

"Wow, nice drive Joe," Jake offered as he sized up their options. "Thank goodness, we can improve our lie. It'd be tough to hit out of there."

As the ball lay, just about any contact would result in it going into the bunker. The smart play would be to hit it out to the side or even backward away from the green. It seems counterintuitive, I know, but often it's the best play. Fortunately, it's a scramble so they can move the ball a few inches, no closer to the pin, and position it on a tuft of grass to assure good contact. A birdie is definitely in play.

"It was your drive, Joe. Chip it in," said Bob. "Save us the trouble."

"Go! Go! Go!" Joe yelled, after his gentle quarter-swing chip shot.

It's quite common for golfers to talk to their golf ball. They all do it. Many actually believe the ball listens. A few even think the ball responds. Those few should probably be somewhere other than on a golf course. You'll also hear them yelling things like "I HATE THIS FREAKING GAME!" or "The golf gods did it to me again." Stay clear of those guys, unless they're in your group, of course. Or, if you happen to be one of them.

"Crap!" Apparently, this isn't one of those times. Joe's ball came up about two inches short of the pin—an easy tap-in for a birdie—but a birdie is not what they wanted. Ironically, a birdie was exactly what they had wanted just a few minutes earlier—on the tee. But, it's not good enough now.

We can talk about greed some other time. It's a common character flaw of most golfers.

Bob hit it fat and chunked it into the bunker, even from his well-positioned lie. I'll talk about overconfidence later, as well.

"God, this is intense," offered Bob. "We really need this one." Bob's short game is pretty solid, but today's pin placement is very difficult considering the slope of the green. He's great at the lob shot. The best strategy from their precarious location next to the bunker, in my opinion, is to hit it a little firm, hit the pin dead on, and drop it in the cup. But, you've got to hit the pin. If that sounds like a lot to ask, you're right. But, it is the best play from here, in my opinion. The only problem with this strategy is if you miss the pin, the ball will roll past the pin, off the front of the green and about twenty yards down the slope in front of the green. This isn't an issue today, however, since they're playing a scramble and they already have one close. For the record, I doubt that today's pin placement was random. Sometimes, the guys that set up the course for a tournament like to mess with you. This is what they call a sucker pin. Most amateur golfers, by nature, are suckers.

Sometimes playing the ball up doesn't solve all of the problems facing a golfer. In this case, there were other factors at play that presented challenges every bit as difficult as the poor lie that playing the ball up mitigated.

"Watch this guys," Jake announced with confidence, as he lined up his clip. His approach was very similar to Joe's—gentle lob shot dying in the cup—he hoped.

"Yes. Yes. YES!" screamed Jake, as he leaped over the bunker and ran toward the cup pumping his fist as if he had just sunk a birdie putt on the 72nd hole to win the U.S, Open—every golfer's dream. "EAGLE!" yelled Jake. "THAT'S AN EAGLE. WOW!"

It took a few minutes for Jake to settle down. The eagle was huge but it alone would not clinch the tournament. It came at a good time, too. The guys had a few minutes on the turn to grab a snack and a beer—or two.

Chapter 6

The Home Stretch

Now on number one, the thirteenth hole of the tournament since their shotgun start on seven, the excitement continued. Jake, without thinking, approached the tee for his drive. In his excitement, he forgot Rick was their lead-off man. He assumed that he had the honor since he'd holed the chip on eighteen for an eagle. He seemed to forget that it was a team effort and that Joe had hit the drive that set up his eagle chip. He took all the credit.

"Rick, we just need to go ahead and retire," suggested Jake. "We could do this every day. Wouldn't that be great? We could all do this every day."

"Hold on there Bobby Jones," Joe interrupted. "I don't know about the rest of you guys, but I've got a few commitments that may limit my play to two or three days a week."

"Oh, come on Joe," said Jake. "If anyone here has the time, and the money for that matter, it's you. I don't mean to downplay the financial wherewithal of Bob and Rick, but you did retire at 55. Money doesn't grow on trees."

Jake's drive, to no one's surprise, wasn't one of his best. The heated discussion about his retirement was apparently beginning to take its toll. Rick, true to form, slammed one down the middle about 210 yards out, leaving a nice approach to the green. Bob pushed his to the right—out of play. Since they still needed to use one of Rick's drives, Joe decided to pass on his drive in an effort to pick up the pace.

"There you go again, Jake. You don't have a clue about retirement. You think it's only about money. Earlier you were whining about all the 'other stuff,' but you don't seem to have given it much thought. If you really want to retire, you need to quit whining and do some research. I think you'll be surprised at what you find."

"For your information, I've done a lot of research about retirement—more than most. In fact, that's all I've read about the past two years. As I said earlier, the financial part is important, obviously, but the key to a 'happy' retirement involves a whole lot more than money. You have to consider what you would be leaving behind— friends, position, prestige, community involvement and corporate activities. If giving up those things concerns you before you retire, you'd better think twice about leaving the job. Or, you'd better find a suitable replacement for them before you do. That's all I'm saying. Those are the concerns that are keeping me up at night."

"You're preaching to the choir, Jake. I've been retired for eight years, remember. Don't you think I had to deal with all of those things? You may have read about them, but I've lived them. Can we play now? We've still got six holes."

"Chill out, Jake," Rick pleaded. "You're getting so uptight about your imminent retirement, it's beginning to affect your game. Can we just concentrate on golf for now, and save the heavy stuff for later?"

"Imminent? What do you mean by imminent? Do you know something I don't know?"

"No, I'm just being realistic. Everybody, except me, plans to retire eventually. I assumed that with all of your talk, and research, you were planning on taking down the shingle soon."

"Just hit the ball Jake, please," Bob pleaded. The group behind them had caught up again and was waiting on the tee box.

Number one at Tempting Slopes is a short par-4, slight dogleg right. Joe's approach shot—best of the group—landed on the back of the green, leaving a very quick putt back down the slope to the front pin position. It'd take two putts for them to get down from there.

Hole number 2 is a short par-3, protected on the front right and front left by large shallow bunkers. Unfortunately, three of the group found them. Only Rick found the putting surface. A two-putt par was the best that anyone could do.

Next up was number three, my favorite hole at Tempting Slopes. It's a long par-5 dogleg left. It'll take three good shots to get to the green, unless you have a gutsy long-hitter in your group, which we do. If he can carry 270, he can hit it over the neighborhood, literally, and land about 150 out. The first order of business is for one of the others to get one in the fairway. If Joe fails to carry the houses, we'll have to play the dogleg, and our chances of a birdie from that distance are greatly reduced.

"Rick, give me some insurance," Joe requested, so he could go for it on his turn. "Long and straight. Aim just left of the juniper tree on the corner and you can take 50 yards off the hole."

"Darn—I pushed it, sorry," Rick apologized. Jake hit his drive too far left and was blocked out by the houses. Bob, feeling the pressure, took a little extra time on his set up. "Slow back—slow through—down the middle," he chanted to himself as he prepared to hit. Positive self-talk never hurt anybody. Not bad—not very long, but it's playable.

"Nice hit Bob," Joe said with an air of relief.

Joe was now free to launch his drive over the neighborhood. All he could think about, for some reason, was that he didn't want to leave it in Jake's backyard. Jake lives on number 3, about 150 yards out, and he gets balls in his backyard often. He's even found balls on his roof—a flat top contemporary design common for this neighborhood when it was built in the 80s. When you take that line, you usually spend four or five minutes looking for the ball once you get to the general landing area. Many are never found. Jake brings us balls all the time from his backyard. Interestingly, they are almost always Titleist Pro V1x brand golf balls. Seems that the guys that think they can hit that far are the same guys that think they need Pro V1x golf balls.

No one said a word as Joe began his setup. Even Jake held his tongue. Joe knew the line— over the chimney of the gray rock house, just left of the giant cottonwood. His nine-and-a-half degree Cobra driver should have the perfect trajectory if he gets it all.

Whack! It's off. Still no comments from the group—just eerie silence.

"Well, Joe?" Jake had to break the silence. "What do you think?"

"I think it might make it," offered Joe with an air of confidence. "I'm not positive, but I hit it good. The line was right. Just hope we can find it."

The challenge with taking the line over the neighborhood is the unknown. It's a blind shot and it's got to be strong. Any slack and it comes up short. Too far right and it's through the fairway into the trees. Too far left and it's in someone's backyard.

Now the fun begins. They'll all drive down to the probable landing area of Joe's drive to look for his ball. If they find it, and it's playable, they're good to go. If not, they'll go back to Bob's drive, way back, and play in from there.

As they curved left at the dogleg and headed down the hill, they strained their eyes to see if they could see Joe's ball in the fairway. Nothing. Bob and Rick went long, past Jake's house, scouring the left rough for a fade. Balls in that area are the hardest to find. The rough is deep and it hides the balls quite well. They turned and headed back up the fairway. Bob couldn't resist a quick glance into Jake's backyard. Still nothing—except his two Chihuahuas.

Joe and Jake went long to see if it had gone through the fairway toward the lake. They'd swing to the right and back up the fifth fairway in case he pushed it. Nothing there either. A quick scan didn't turn up anything so they'd backtrack, slow down a bit, and look a little closer. They have five minutes, according to the rules, to search for a lost ball. They'd exhausted three already.

"Here it is," yelled Jake. "Awesome drive, Joe."

Just in time. Only about a minute to spare, assuming someone was actually timing.

Joe's ball came to rest through the fairway in the right rough. The rough is cut pretty tight on that side of the fairway, so that won't be a factor. The problem from that location can be the trees. In a scramble format, they can move the ball a foot or two, so getting around a trunk won't be an issue, but getting around or over the rest of the tree will call for some creative shot-making.

Bob and Rick pulled up to where Joe and Jake were waiting after retrieving Bob's ball. They left it lying where it landed just in case they didn't find Joe's ball and had to play it.

"How's it look, guys?" queried Bob. "Do we have an opening?"

"Not too bad," offered Joe, in his normal confident tone.

"Easy for you to say. Let me restate the question. Do WE have an opening?"

"Yeah, I think so," said Joe. "You'll need to turn it a little bit to get to the green, but it's doable."

"We're 147 out guys," Jake shared, as he read off the yardage from his trusty Bushnell rangefinder. "I'll hit first. I've got a mean fade and it might just work here. I'll cut my 7-wood just left of the tree, toward that white house, and hope it turns."

Jake's ball did fade. It generally does, whether he wants it to or not. And, sometimes the fade serves him well. Other times, not so much. On this occasion, however, it did as he had hoped and came to rest just left of the green. Bob hit next. He tried to draw it around the right side of the tree but it didn't cooperate and ended up in the lake.

"Rick, you're up. (pause) Rick, you gonna hit? (pause) RICK!" Jake raised his voice to get Rick's attention. Rick had slipped into a daze. That had happened several times during the round and was beginning to worry the others.

"Something's just not right with Rick," Jake whispered to Joe. "I hope the cancer hasn't come back. He saw his doctor again last week. I wish he'd open up."

"He will … eventually," said Joe. "When he's ready."

Rick took the route left of the tree as well. Most amateurs have a cut shot in their bag, or rather a slice. The key is controlling it. He didn't get quite the turn he was hoping for and ended up about 40 yards left of the green.

"Sorry guys," Rick offered.

Joe was next up and their last and best chance of getting on the green. If they could get anywhere on the green, a birdie was a real possibility.

"Easy Joe," Jake insisted.

"Yes coach," Joe said in a sarcastic tone.

"Sorry."

Joe chose a line left of the tree as well, coming to rest just off the left fringe. They'd be chipping, but it's a difficult up and down from there. Lots of break to the right. From that distance, a two-putt birdie is no guarantee.

"If we can get down in two from here, we're definitely in the money," Jake said. "Last year's winning score was eleven under, but with today's wind, I think a nine or ten under will be hard to beat."

"Yes Jake, we know," Bob said, with a bit of a snarl in his voice. Their camaraderie seemed to be waning, at least as it related to Jake and his incessant commentary. Hopefully, they can keep it together for a few more holes.

Rick chipped first and was closest to the pin of the group—on his second try. They each had one mulligan for the tournament, and, unfortunately, used them all, hoping for another eagle. Rick tapped his in for a birdie. They were now standing at nine-under with three holes to play.

Number 4 at Tempting Slopes is a sharp dogleg right around a small lake. Joe, and possibly Bob with today's wind, had enough distance to cut the corner, but it'd take a good hit. The carry to clear the water from today's tee placement is about 190 yards.

Rick, as usual, hit his drive down the middle. Safe, but a good 155 to the back pin. They needed to get one closer to improve their chances of a birdie. Bob tried to cut the corner but came up just short and in the lake. Jake tried desperately to improve on Rick's drive, but came up short and left leaving at least 170 to the pin. Joe, our "A" player, came through again, cleared the lake and rolled down the slope to a nice flat lie 40 yards or so from the green. From there, they'd need a good pitch to have a chance for a birdie. The pin placement was in a very difficult location and just about every attempt to get close runs off the back of the green. They needed to land about 30 feet short and run it up to get close. After four attempts, the closest to the pin was about twelve feet—not as close as they had hoped for, but up hill. Not too difficult but certainly not a gimme.

Things were getting serious now. Everyone was quiet while their teammates were putting. They really wanted to finish strong. A birdie here would be huge. Bob putted first, hitting his ball pretty firm up the hill. He had a good line but hit a little too hard running about two feet past the hole.

Jake, heeding the lesson of Bob's putt, left his putt about a foot short—a great putt but not the birdie they needed. Rick was still in his golf cart, so Joe would putt next.

"Rick, are you planning on putting here?" Jake yelled. "I'm telling you guys, something is wrong with Rick. He's been in La La Land all day."

Rick hurried to the green, but he was too late. Joe slammed his putt into the back of the hole—center cut. Rick's attempt was not needed. Ten-under with two to play.

Holes 5 and 6, the final two holes for the group, would offer them little chance of lowering their score any further. Looks like ten-under will be their final score in the clubhouse. Both holes are long and offer some challenging aspects that can catch an unsuspecting player off guard. Their goal for the final two holes was to not do worse than par. With Rick in suspended animation and Jake stressed to a point of barely knowing where he was, it would be up to Joe and Bob to bring it home. Fortunately, Joe was driving the ball as well as anyone of the guys had ever seen. His approach shots were solid as well. Bob hadn't contributed much on the drives or approach shots, but his short game had been spot on all day. Between the two of them, and a little help from Rick and Jake, they managed to get to the clubhouse at ten-under. Not too bad for today's conditions. Now they wait.

"Congratulations guys," Jake proclaimed as he began the round of handshakes, as he always does. "Great round! Can't wait to see where we stand."

They were anxious to post their score but decided to put their clubs away first. Rick threw his clubs in the back of his pickup and decided to head on home. He wasn't the least bit interested in their standing. He probably didn't even know their final score. The others stopped by the locker room to freshen up before posting their score.

"Anyone beat ten-under? Jake queried the club pros as they entered the banquet room where everyone was congregating following their rounds. That's where lunch would be served and the prizes would be handed out. "We're going to need a big table for all of our winnings."

"Ten-under?" Butch, the head pro at Tempting Slopes and today's designated score checker, asked for confirmation.

"Yep—ten, read my lips, ten, ten-under."

"Wow, not bad for a bunch of old duffers. What were you guys drinking?"

"Sandbaggers!" Shouts came from several parts of the room.

Anyone that came in that low was a target for insults—especially old duffers. Only about half of the scores had been posted at that point, so they'd have to wait a while to know their ultimate fate. Time for a beer.

With seven scores posted, they were in the lead, but that could change at any time. The Blanchard group was still out. They won last year, and the year before that. The Vanlandingham group was still out, as well. They had racked up several tournaments this year and were expected to do well today. Jake's Raiders, aptly named following their blockbuster round today, could drop out of the money at any moment.

"Here they come," announced Jake, as the Vanlandingham group approached the clubhouse. "I'm going to croak if they beat our ten-under."

"I'll pull my car around now, chided Bill Vanlandingham as he entered the banquet room. "Can I get some help loading the trophy?"

"Not so fast, Bill," Joe interrupted. "How'd you guys do? Can you beat ten-under?"

"Ten-under! No way. Not with today's conditions."

"Yeah. Ten-under. Read it and weep."

"Wow! Impressive. Congratulations. What were you guys drinking? I doubt anyone beats that."

"Why does everyone think our low score was the result of what we were drinking?" asked Jake. "Can't you just accept the fact that today we were the best team?"

"Not so fast Jake. Blanchard's still out," noted Butch. "If anyone can beat your ten-under, it's his group."

"Here comes Blanchard now," Jake interrupted. "They look disappointed. I think we won. I'm sure we won."

Frank Blanchard was last in his group to enter the banquet room. They all looked disappointed as they approached the scoring table. Frank tossed their scorecard on the table and continued on to the keg without so much as a nod. The suspense was killing everyone, especially Jake.

"Well, Frank. What's the verdict?" asked Jake.

"Don't know—didn't total it up. Just another round."

The suspense was too much for Jake. He got up and went over to the scoring table to find out for himself. Frank wasn't kidding, they really hadn't totaled up their score. Butch was frantically tallying, checking and rechecking. Everyone was waiting. It was a little hard to believe so he checked it one more time.

"Ten-under," Butch announced, as Frank sipped calmly from his freshly drawn lager.

"Ten-under?" questioned Jake. "Crap. What do we do now? How do we break the tie, Butch?"

"Scorecard playoff. Or a duel at sunset between the two team captains," Butch joked. "What's your pleasure gentlemen?"

"I hate scorecard playoffs." Jake reeled in disgust. "It's crazy to work so hard for the win only to have the outcome decided by scorecard roulette. We came here to play golf. Why can't we decide the winner by who plays the best round? Who decided to use scorecard playoff to break a tie, anyway?"

"I did," offered Butch. "We always use scorecard playoffs to break ties. No one wants to hang around after a tournament any longer than it takes to scarf down a burger and drink a beer."

"I say we break the tie with a real playoff," suggested Jake. Anyone else game, or are you all wimps?"

"Butch," Frank interrupted. "I never have liked scorecard playoffs either. I'm with Jake. I say we have a real playoff for a change."

"It doesn't make me any difference. I'm here 'til dark, regardless. But, to be fair, I think everyone should agree. The scorecard playoff is in the rules. To change it after the tournament will require a unanimous vote of everyone on both teams."

"Sounds good to me. Let's vote," insisted Jake.

"Wait a minute," Butch insisted. "We first need to decide how the playoff will take place. I suggest all members of both teams huddle up and try to come up with something. Something that everyone can agree on."

"Problem!" Joe interrupted. "One of our members has already left."

It bears mentioning at this point that nothing in life is ever simple. The rules governing a tie were clear. Everyone knew them. The simple solution would have been to just follow the rules. That said, Jake and the others had a point. A scorecard playoff is a bit like holding an election for president and deciding the outcome based on who has the ugliest dog. I too am an advocate of deciding the winner of a golf tournament by, well, playing golf. The scorecard playoff was concocted as a quick and easy method for breaking ties in golf tournaments because, it was assumed by someone, that everyone was in a hurry to leave. I suspect if you took a vote, you'd find most of the guys in today's tournament weren't in any hurry to leave—after all, the beer is free as long as it lasts. If you've set aside time in your schedule to play a tournament, include enough time, and a logical method, for breaking ties. That, to me, is simple.

Hidden in the debate that was transpiring in the clubhouse regarding the tie, is a much bigger problem with society as a whole. Everyone is in a hurry, all the time. Just look at today's round. To begin with, there's a rule that says that a round of golf should take no longer than four hours and fifteen minutes, and to make sure that none do, a marshal is timing your progress around the course. There's a rule that you can look for a lost ball for no more than five minutes, after which a penalty will be imposed. Once your round is complete, you are instructed to proceed immediately to the clubhouse to post your score, because everyone is waiting. Butch was in a hurry to verify and post the scores. Everyone was in a hurry to eat lunch.

And, Jake was just in a hurry. Why not slow down and enjoy life, and golf, a little more.

The members of the two teams that were tied at ten-under crowded around a table to discuss options for breaking the tie. One player suggested a putt off. Another, a chip off. Still another, a sudden death playoff beginning on hole number one. Most thought the first two suggestions were too brief and offered little advantage over the scorecard playoff. One putt or one chip shouldn't determine the winner of an eighteen-hole tournament. The sudden death idea garnered some support, but a few thought it favored the group that just came in, over the team that had been in the clubhouse for a while, had eaten lunch and had a few beers. This option was also complicated by Rick's earlier departure. After some grumbling by a couple of old codgers that were ready to go home, and some shrewd negotiating by the team captains, they finally decided that they'd play a three-hole playoff, followed by a putt-off if they were still tied. Each team would be represented by two members of their choice so there'd be only one group to follow. And, for a little added excitement, it'd be played head-to-head, scratch, to eliminate the possibility of someone sandbagging.

Everyone would play their own ball and they'd play it down. The combined score of each team's two players would determine the winner of the tournament. It was time to vote. Jake called Rick, but he did not answer his phone. Butch waived the requirement for Rick's input so the vote was unanimous. They'd play a three-hole playoff. Fortunately, it was early and there was still plenty of time to get in the three additional holes. Most of the guys were excited and looked forward to watching the playoff.

Chapter 7

The Playoff

After a twenty minute break to warm up and hit a few range balls, the two teams met on the number one tee box, drew numbers to see who'd lead off, and played away. The teams consisted of Joe and Jake versus Frank and Gene Billings since their handicaps matched up well. Joe and Frank both have a five handicap while Jake and Gene have 15 and 16 handicaps respectively—close enough.

Frank drew the number one, so he'd lead off, followed by Gene.

Frank's drive was down the middle and about 260 out, about what you'd expect for a five handicap player. Gene pushed his drive a little right, about 210 out.

"That's the best you've got guys," Jake chided.

"That's all we need, Jake. I've seen your drive," Frank responded in kind.

Looks like the playoff is going to be spiced up a bit with a little trash talk. Never a dull minute with these guys.

Joe wanted Jake to hit first so he'd know whether to hit full out or baby it down the fairway.

Jake, feeling a little nervous with a gallery, hit his drive a little thin. It barely got off the ground, landed about 150 out, and rolled another 20 yards, coming to rest about 190 yards from the pin. Jake would be fortunate to end up with a bogey with a start like that. Joe was going to have to play aggressive—looks like he might be carrying Jake.

Joe's drive was long, about 280, and just off the fairway in the first cut. The left rough was just long enough to provide a nice pad for the ball, and the angle from Joe's location was perfect.

Tournament playoffs are always more stressful than the tournament itself. At that point, you're close to winning, but it's not in the bag yet. But, losing a playoff is worse than losing outright, especially with everyone watching. Stress from any source does interesting things to one's psyche, and golf tournaments, particularly playoffs, are no exception.

Jake didn't give it much thought when they negotiated the playoff rules, but he was about to get a lesson he'd not soon forget. As you may recall from the earlier chapters, Jake liked to play the ball up—improving his lie. He's about to face golf, and life for that matter, head on.

As Jake approached his ball, he noticed that it had come to rest in a divot. Not thinking, his initial response was to nudge it out of the divot with the head of his 3-wood, the club he'd chosen for his approach shot.

"What are you doing, Jake?" Frank asked. "We're playing the ball down."

"Oh crap, I forgot. What do I do now?"

"You replace the ball in the divot. Plus, it's a one stroke penalty," Gene recited the rules, to the best of his memory.

"Are you sure? If I declare it 'unplayable,' wouldn't I just take a drop, and incur a one stroke penalty? I don't have to put it back in the divot, do I?"

"I'm not sure. Let's call Butch."

Butch confirmed Gene's initial interpretation of the rule that applied. For an unplayable lie, Jake would have had to have declared it unplayable before he touched the ball. And, quite honestly, it'd be a bit of a stretch declaring a ball in a divot an unplayable lie.

Jake's just not cut out for tournament play, at least not serious tournament play. He never plays the ball down, so his handicap is bogus, to his disadvantage. He gets stressed out too easily, about anything, about everything. Stress and competition simply do not mix. In fact, stress doesn't mix well with anything. There are those who claim that stress is necessary for performing at the highest level. I contend, however, that it's not simply stress that propels one's performance, leading to great success, but rather their management of the stress. Sort of like rocket fuel—a controlled explosion, with emphasis on the control. Otherwise, the destructive force is just that, destructive. In Jake's case, he's an active carrier of stress, but a poor manager—not a good combination in golf, or in life.

Jake took a minute to compose himself after his unintended breach of the rules. Now, he's fretting over having to hit his ball out of the divot.

"Here goes nothing. I don't think I've ever actually hit a ball out of a divot. Keep your eye on it, Joe. God only knows where it'll end up."

"Don't give up yet, Jake," consoled Joe as he prepared for his third hit. "It's just the first hole." You could tell Jake was nervous—he waggled his 3-wood about 40 times before hitting.

"Nice hit, Jake, considering the lie. You can do this."

"Where'd it go? I was afraid to look."

"Short right. Near the cart path. See it?"

"If this is what retirement's like, I think I'll keep working. Maybe Bob's work-until-you-die plan isn't such a bad idea, after all." When Jake gets nervous, he tries to think about something else. In fact, he can't help himself.

"So, you're thinking about retirement," said Joe, trying to get Jake's mind off the game. The diversion sounds counterintuitive, but he had to do something or Jake would implode.

"I'd love to. I just don't know if I can pull the plug."

"Pull the plug," questioned Joe. "What do you mean, pull the plug?"

"You know. Hang up the spurs, take down the old shingle—pull the plug. I just don't know if I can walk away from the paycheck. It's too easy to just keep on going to work, put in my 40 hours, and go home."

"You said earlier that it wasn't about money. You said you were okay financially. What's a paycheck got to do with it?"

"Nothing really—it's just hard to walk away and leave the paycheck lying there on the desk. I find myself calculating how many more months I'd have to work to buy me a new car before I retire, or how many more months I'd have to work to buy Julie a new car, or a golf cart, or a…, it never ends. How did you walk away eight years ago, Joe?"

They were so deeply engrossed in their conversation, they hadn't even noticed that Gene and Frank had both hit their second shot. It was Joe's turn. He was only about 80 yards out, so it'd be a full wedge for him.

Joe's plan to distract Jake was working well. So well, in fact, that neither had a clue what had transpired thus far. Joe knew he needed a good pitch and a 2-putt for his par, but he failed to keep track of Jake's hits. Unfortunately, Jake chunked his fourth shot, chipped to the front of the green, and two-putted for a seven. They had no idea where they stood.

"What'd you get, guys?" asked Jake. "We kind of lost count."

"Par for me," offered Frank "and a bogey for Gene."

Joe and Jake were two down after the first playoff hole. Jake's nerves, and his lack of experience playing the ball down, had taken a toll early.

Number 2 is a short par-3, protected on the front right and front left by shallow bunkers. The safe hit is to go long so you'll clear the bunkers if your drive is a little wayward. But, with the front pin position, long doesn't bode well if you want a birdie, which they desperately needed.

"You still have the honor, Frank," Jake was quick to point out.

Frank had a beautiful shot, high with a soft landing about twelve feet right of the pin. This hole is a lot easier if you can hit a seven or eight iron from the tee. Gene, however, needed a little more club, so he hit his 7-hybrid, landing on the back of the green—safe, but a long way from the hole.

Jake hit his 6-iron about ten yards short of the green, avoiding the bunkers. I think that was probably his strategy. When he gets in a bunker, he usually spends some time there. His second shot was an easy chip for most golfers, but Jake and his pitching wedge don't always get along too well. He's tried every technique that's been published in

Golfers Digest and none of them have worked for him. He even bought a used Dunlop Solution Flop Wedge last year that was "guaranteed to solve all your chipping and bunker problems." Didn't happen. It's no wonder he always plays the ball up. Guess that's okay in friendly rounds, but it'll destroy your game if you ever intend to play in tournaments or leagues that follow USGA rules. He'll putt in this case—that's the second part of his strategy.

Joe stepped up to the tee, tossed his ball down, moved it around a little with his eight iron to get a good lie, took one practice swing, and hit away. No tee. No strain. Smooth as silk.

"Nice shot," Frank said, as Joe's ball landed just behind the pin and stopped dead. Everyone, except Jake, jumped into their cart and moved on to the green. Jake walked the short distance to his drive.

Jake reached his ball first and putted from off the green, ran it a ways past the pin, and two-putted for a bogey. Gene three-putted for a bogey. Frank two-putted for a par. And, Joe tapped in for a birdie, trimming Frank's and Gene's lead to one.

"So, Joe, how did you walk away eight years ago?" Jake continued.

"How? Well, it occurred to me that the only difference between retiring at the time and working longer was the amount of money that would be in my bank account when I died," Joe said as he pulled away from the second green.

"Do what?" Jake wondered if he'd missed something. "What do you mean?"

"Exactly what I said. Listen closely, I'll speak slowly. I realized the only difference between retiring at the time and working longer was the amount of money that'd be in my bank account when I died. In other works, whether I retired eight years ago, two years ago or ten years from now, my lifestyle wouldn't change. Life would go on as usual. The only difference, literally, would be the value of my estate when I died. How much I'd leave to my kids."

"Wow. I never thought of it that way. That certainly gives you a different perspective. That's for sure."

"Last hole," announced Gene. "I believe it's your honor, guys."

Joe had given Jake a lot to think about. So much so that he was having a hard time concentrating on the playoff. His tee shot didn't quite make it to the dogleg and landed in the left rough behind some shrubs. From there, his only option was to punch it out into the fairway.

Considering Jake's drive, Joe was a little nervous about cutting off too much of the corner. The neighborhood looked very uninviting, knowing that Jake was looking at a bogey at best. But without a birdie from Joe, it didn't much matter. Surely Frank would get at least a par and Gene probably a bogey. A birdie could put us in a sudden death. Without it, it's over. He's got no choice.

"This is it, Jake. All or nothing." Whack!

"Looking good. Same line as the last time, maybe a little more left. Hope it carries."

"We'll know soon," assured Joe, as he slid his driver back into his bag for the final time in the tournament.

"So, Jake, now that I've shared with you the secret that makes the retirement decision a whole lot easier, are you ready to set a date?"

"Huh—not hardly. There's still all of the other stuff I mentioned earlier."

"Oh yeah, the other stuff," quipped Joe. "What were those again?'

"Purpose, camaraderie, position, structure—the things I'd be giving up," repeated Jake.

"We already scratched camaraderie from your list, remember. You have no friends at work, trust me. Once you retire, they'll forget you like the burnt toast they had for breakfast. As for purpose or position, honestly, those things never really changed for me. Everyone that respected me for what I did in my job continued to respect me after I retired. In fact, even more so now. I think getting to the end of a distinguished career with your integrity intact carries over into retirement. Doctors are still referred to as doctors. Same for judges, military veterans, even politicians. I think you'll find that the same thing applies to you, just without the title."

''Makes sense," said Jake. "So much of the adjustment is mental. It's about understanding the transition, accepting that it is a normal part of life, and convincing yourself that it's the best thing for you—for me—when all the other stars line up."

"As for structure," Joe continued, "You'll still have structure. It'll just be a different structure. You'll soon find that the morning routine of making coffee, checking emails, rummaging through the inbox, and checking the sales figures for the previous day will be replaced by other things, better things, more rewarding things—

things that benefit you and your family, not the boss and the stockholders. My advice to you regarding structure is simple: Don't worry about it, it'll come. Don't try to force it. Once you pull the plug, take a few weeks, maybe even a few months, to soak in the new you. You're retired! You've spent 45 to 50 years of your life 'working' for the benefit of others. It's time to 'play' for the benefit of you. Structure will come soon enough. I promise."

"Hit your ball, Jake."

Jake pitched out of the rough and skulled his third shot about thirty yards down the fairway.

"Darn it. I did it again," Jake grumbled as he walked down the slope to his ball.

Jake's problem, if you haven't figured it out by now, is his lack of experience hitting a golf ball under normal conditions. As we've covered many times previously, he always moves his ball to a tuft of grass, away from obstacles, and out of bunkers, so he'll have an easy hit. He plays it up. When he has to hit the ball from a down position, he can't. He's never, almost never, done that. When it really matters, like today, he just can't perform the way he'd like. It's a different game—one he's not played before. And, to make things even worse, his handicap is based on hitting the ball from ideal positions, so he starts out five or six strokes down.

Gene hit his second shot about 120 yards short of the green. Frank's ball was in the fairway about 150 out. They still hadn't found Joe's ball.

"Here it is, Joe," Gene shouted after finding Joe's ball in the left rough. He was only about 130 out and in the open, so he'd have a good chance at getting his second shot close.

"An eagle would sure be nice," Joe whispered to himself. A little self-talk never hurts in situations like this.

Joe got his eagle, but it wasn't good enough. Jake got on in five and three-putted for an eight. They were four over for the playoff.

Gene hit his fourth onto the green and two-putted for a bogey six. Frank only needed a bogey to win the match for his team. His third shot was on the left front of the green, about 30 feet from the pin. A two-putt from there would be good enough, and that he did—giving them a final score of two over for the playoff, winning by two.

After the round, everyone shook hands and headed back to the clubhouse. Everyone agreed that the three hole playoff was a great idea. It sure added an extra measure of excitement to the day. I think it's safe to say it'll be the norm in the future.

Chapter 8

Conclusion

"Nice round, Joe," Jake offered, as they cut across the fifth fairway on their way back to the clubhouse. "Sorry I let you down, and the team."

"You didn't let anybody down, Jake. It's a game. We were here to have fun. I had a great time, and I hope you did too. My gosh, we took second place—that's a hundred bucks each. How's that letting anyone down? When we get to the clubhouse, let's have a beer and figure out what we need to do to get you retired."

"Sounds good," Jake said, feeling a little better following Joe's words of encouragement.

On the way back to the clubhouse, Jake called Rick to give him the news. When Rick left earlier, nobody knew anything. Half the field was still on course, and the playoff wasn't even a consideration yet.

"Hello, Rick. This is Jake. How are you feeling guy? We were worried about you."

"Oh, hi Jake," Rick replied, in a somber tone of voice. "I'm fine. Sorry I cut out early. I was really tired after the tournament."

"No problem. I just wanted to let you know the outcome. After the match, we were tied at 10-under with Frank Blanchard's team. Nobody wanted to settle it with scorecard roulette, so we had a three hole playoff. Unfortunately, we lost the playoff, and took second place—100 bucks coming your way, man."

"Wow. That's great. Nice job, Jake. Tell Joe and Bob I said congrats."

"I will," assured Jake. (pause) "Are you sure you're okay, Rick? You've got us worried."

Joe dropped Jake off at the men's locker room entrance, returned the cart to the cart barn, and went on to the banquet room for the awards presentation. Jake went in the locker room to continue the phone conversation with Rick in private.

"I'm fine," Rick said. "I've been better. I just haven't been feeling a hundred percent lately. There's a lot going on right now, and I can't seem to keep all the plates spinning, so to speak."

"Plates spinning?" queried Jake. "What plates?"

"You know, 'plates...spinning.' I just can't seem to keep up with everything anymore—the job, the house, the kids, the grandkids, and now the great-grandkids. I don't ever seem to have time for me anymore. I know, it sounds selfish, I admit it. But my health hasn't been the greatest the past few years, as you know, and I don't want to die before I have an opportunity to enjoy life a little more, for me and Roxanne both to enjoy life (pause) a little more. All of your talk about retirement the past few weeks really got me thinking. I've worked for DHS for 31 years. I think I need to borrow some of your books on retirement and figure out how I can put that place behind."

"Wow. I've been really worried about you the past few weeks, Rick. I was afraid your cancer had returned. Sounds to me like you just need to figure out a way to retire too. I never thought the decision to retire was so complicated. Seems it's a more common dilemma that I thought."

"Cancer—no. The T-cell count is still good. Can we get together in the next week or so? I'd sure like to hear more about all of your retirement planning, everything you've learned, books you can recommend. I think you may be right. I think I do need to retire."

"Absolutely," assured Jake, as they concluded their conversation. "Call me."

"Congratulations on the tournament, Jake. How do I get my hundred bucks?"

By the time Jake joined the others at the awards presentation, Butch had totaled up the scores and announced the winners. Frank's team took first. Joe's team took second. Third place went to Bill Vanlandingham's team.

"Let's get a beer, guys. I'll buy," offered Joe. "So, Jake, have we addressed all of your concerns about retirement, or are there still things lingering? It can't be money anymore, not with your winnings today."

"Ha! We just talked about the things I'd be leaving behind. We didn't even touch on the things I'd be facing."

"Facing? What do you mean, facing?"

"Well, if you believe what's on the Internet, the biggest issues among new retirees are depression, loneliness, too much 'up close and personal time' with the spouse, and lack of motivation to do anything, even getting out of bed. If you can come up with a solution for those things, I'm good to go."

"That's easy. Stay off the Internet," joked Bob.

"Here's the thing Jake," Joe said, in his most serious tone yet. "You're a good friend, so I'm going to level with you. It may be simpler than you think. You're right about the finances. That's not the only thing to consider. But, it's a pretty darned important one. If you can't meet your financial obligations, nothing else matters much. I trust that you're okay in that department. That's what you said earlier—right. Everything else, in my humble opinion, is negotiable. What I mean by that, is that the things you are giving up—position, structure, purpose—are either irrelevant or can be replaced by other things equally as important to you. But that's your choice. It's an important decision, but one that you, and only you, can make. You may have to learn how to let go of some things.

"As for the things you'll be 'facing,' to use your own term, they're negotiable as well, to some extent. The things that would worry me the most are depression, loneliness, feelings of worthlessness, that sort of thing. They're real and if you can't control them on your own, through your own actions and by building a social network outside of work, then you may need to seek professional help. I don't have a silver bullet for those. But, I can assure you that they are real and they are issues that retirees face more often than not. They can destroy your retirement, but they don't have to. As for the 'up close and personal' challenge of both you and Julie being retired, I have a simple solution for that too. The key to a couple coexisting successfully in retirement is to live separate lives, together. Make sense?"

"Sort of, but it doesn't sound so easy to me."

"I didn't say it would be easy. I said it would be simple. You guys have gotten along great for over forty years, best I can tell. The only difference is that you'll be spending a few more hours together each day. 'Live separate lives, together."

Joe had never talked to Jake quite like that. It was clear that Joe was speaking from his heart, giving advice and sharing personal experiences he'd encountered since his retirement eight years earlier. It felt good to be in the 'retirement planning' business again. It brought great memories of his long-time career of helping couples realize their dreams. Joe also made it clear that Jake, and Jake alone, would ultimately be the architect of his own fate.

"Jake, the important thing for you to do right now is to talk to Julie. Discuss your concerns—

they're her concerns, as well. Everything that you will encounter—the things you'll be leaving behind as well as the things you'll be facing going forward—can be dealt with. It reminds me of something I was told many times growing up—probably you too. 'If you fail to plan, then you plan to fail.' Same concept. People who go blindly into retirement, without adequate and timely preparation, may be surprised at what they find. It's incumbent upon you to find a solution for every one of your concerns, preferably before you retire. However, for some of those concerns, a perfect solution may not exist, in which case you'll have to decide the best course based on the best information you can get. And, you may have to compromise.

"What is so abundantly clear to me today, and it gets clearer every day, is that my decision to retire eight years ago was without question the right decision for me. I was okay financially, and I thought that was all that mattered. I didn't find out about all that other stuff—the things I'd be giving up and the things I'd be facing—until they hit me head on, like a ton of bricks. I addressed them one at a time. Some things were pretty simple to work out—other things, not so much. You're doing the right thing, Jake, checking into everything before hand. But, don't make yourself crazy worrying about every minute detail. Do your research. Develop your plan. Execute. And, live the good life."

"But, what if I make the wrong decision?" Jake asked. "What if the stock market crashes and our IRA loses half its value? What if Julie or I get real sick, heaven forbid, and we exhaust our finances. What if..."

"Hold it right there," Joe interrupted. "Now you're being paranoid again. That's where the plan comes in. If it makes you feel better, set down with Julie and run through all the scenarios you can think of, but just the ones that are real possibilities. Save the zombie attacks and the giant man-eating spiders for Steven Spielberg. Soon, you'll have a clearer idea of how to plan for just about anything that could happen. But, you've got to have a plan."

"King."

"Excuse me?"

"It's Steven King, not Spielberg," Jake corrected Joe.

"Life's too short, man. There's so much to do out there and so little time to do it. None of us know how much time we've been given on this great planet. Don't spend it all worrying about the next big disaster. Make a plan, execute, and live the good life. Let's go home."

Acknowledgements

This book would not have been possible without the talented input and dedicated support of my family and friends. I would first like to thank my wife, **Barbara**, for being my 'alpha' reviewer. She was first to read my manuscript and was brutally honest in her suggestions, all of which were excellent and kept me grounded.

I would also like to thank our good friends **Jeanie and Allen Vance**, for their excellent editorial skills and 'beta' reviewer input. They brought unique insights to the process in the areas of education, management, retirement and golf.

To my brother **Steve**, master researcher and author of *Indian Trade Silver Markings*, and his wife **Ginger** for their excellent proofreading and editing skills.

And, finally, to **Jason Matthews**, author of *How to Make, Market and Sell EBooks*, who inspired me to give self-publishing a try, for his guidance and support.

Glossary

ADDRESSING THE BALL – Standing upright, facing the ball, preparing to swing the club.

APPROACH SHOT – A hit to the green.

BIG DOG – A slang term for the driver.

BIRD or BIRDIE – A score of one-under par on a hole.

BOGIE – A score of one-over par on a hole.

BUNKER – Sand trap.

CARDING – Entering your score on your scorecard.

CLEAN HIT – Striking the golf ball with the golf club without the interference of grass, sand or other obstruction.

DIVOT – A sliver of turf (damage) that is cut away when hit by a golf club during the swing.

DRAW – A slight, often controlled, curve of the golf ball to the left following the hit (right-handed golfer).

DUFFER – An amateur golfer who plays golf too infrequently to become very good at the game.

EAGLE – A score of two-under par on a hole.

FADE – A slight, often controlled, curve of the golf ball to the right following the hit (right-handed golfer).

FOOT WEDGE – When a golfer looks around to make sure no one is watching and kicks his golf ball into a more playable position.

FOURSOME – A group of four golfers playing together.

FOUR-MAN SCRAMBLE – A game of golf consisting of teams of four playing a scramble format. (see SCRAMBLE)

GIMME – A short putt, so rarely missed that many golfers concede it to their opponents.

HONOR – The privilege of hitting the first tee shot on a hole, extended to a player for performance on the previous hole that exceeded that of his or her opponents.

MULLIGAN – An extra hit, used in place of a poor hit, usually agreed to or purchased before a round begins.

NASSAU– A variation of golf in which the players wager an equal amount of money on their score for the front nine, their score for the back nine, and their total score for eighteen holes.

PAR – The number of shots a scratch golfer is expected to take on a hole.

PLAY IT DOWN – Playing a golf ball as it lies.

PLAY IT UP – Moving a golf ball within a designated distance, typically the length of the grip on a golf club, to improve one's lie away from a divot, a tree root, or another obstacle.

POND – Slang for water hazard.

PULL – Hitting the golf ball further to the left than intended (right-handed person).

PUSH – Hitting the golf ball further to the right than intended (right-handed person).

REGULATION – Reaching a green in the appropriate number of hits, i.e. two on a par-4 or three on a par-5.

SAND SAVE – Hitting the ball out of the sand trap, followed by a one-putt into the hole.

SANDBAGGER – A derogatory term applied to a golfer who cheats by pretending to be worse than he or she really is in order to raise his or her handicap, thus giving him or her an unfair advantage during official play.

SANDY LIE – The lie of a golf ball that comes to rest in a sand trap.

SCRAMBLE – A variation of golf in which all golfers on a team hit their ball from the same location (typically the best location).

SHOTGUN START – A starting procedure in a golf tournament in which all teams start at the same designated time, but from different holes.

SLICE – Curving a golf ball further to the right than planned or expected (right-handed golfer).

SUCKER PIN – A pin placement on a green that entices a golfer to hit his ball to a difficult location.

SWEET SPOT – the place on the face of the golf club that has been engineered to produce the most efficient and effective launch of the golf ball when struck by the golf club at the bottom of the downswing—the impact.

TAP IN – A short putt.

THE TURN – The transition between the ninth green and the tenth tee on a typical golf course. A great opportunity to grab a refreshment.

UNPLAYABLE LIE – When a ball that is in play comes to rest in a location or position from which it cannot be played.

About the Author

Dave Cox, upon retiring from a long and rewarding career in public service, set aside plans he had made for his much anticipated 'free time' to document the many and varied adventures (and diversions) that he encountered (and endured) over the course of his adult life. His formal education in Management, Human Resources, and Computer Science guided him along a successful path with long engagements in urban planning and public health, both of which are sure to inspire later writings that need to be shared, but his diversions into treasure hunting, golf, travel, and other interests provided fodder for this and other books in various stages of completion.

For more information about Dave Cox and CoxQuest Publishing, go to CoxQuest.com.

Afterward

Thank you for reading my book. It was a pleasure sharing it with you. If you enjoyed it, it would mean a great deal to me if you would leave a review on Amazon.com. Only through feedback from readers like you am I able to improve my craft and expand my offerings.

If you would like to preview my forthcoming books, please go to CoxQuest.com and click on the 'PUBLISHING' tab in the Main Menu.

Thanks,
Dave

Printed in Great Britain
by Amazon